spaces of serenity
small projects for meditation & contemplation

Jeffery S. Poss

ORO
EDITIONS

*Wabi is to be satisfied with a little hut,
a room of two or three tatami mats, like
the log cabin of Thoreau.*
                                    —Daisetz T. Suzuki

*If architects…were existentially rather
than "success" oriented – we would,
with some regularity, see at least some
architects designing progressively smaller and smaller structures as their careers
developed over time.*
                                    —Leonard Koren

Introduction

In 1989, I moved from Connecticut back to Central Illinois to teach at the state's flagship institution and begin a small private architectural practice. I was returning to the place where I trained a decade earlier in order to renew my fascination with the region's seemingly limitless landscape. I wanted to explore the gestalt relationships between elemental constructed forms, the intensely horizontal ground, and the large, open sky.

Among these explorations were ideas for private habitation as built landscape. An initial example is "Prospect and Refuge," (previous pages) a study from 1991 that proposes an essential dwelling emerging from a vast landscape. The surrounding sloped ground merges up into the structure in a seamless composition.

The following year, "House for a Subdivision" (far left) transferred this idea to a residential neighborhood. Again, the idea was to simultaneously shape the earth form and the architectural form. The center of the composition became a vertical circulation shaft that acted as an "axis mundi," a symbolic connection between ground and sky. At the pinnacle of this shaft was a space with extensive views, a "proto-hut," a small space at the top of several steps for meditation and observation (top left). Following this study, I became intrigued with this idea of designing spaces specifically attuned to meditation, mindfulness, and creative contemplation.

The resulting projects have explored the creation of these small spaces, separated from the other residential program activities to sustain a serene atmosphere. This separation has been achieved either by locating this space on a prominent level above other residential activities, or by creating a separate detached "hut."

The first of these projects began when my soon-to-be-wife Barbara Diller-Young moved from Connecticut to join me in Illinois. We lived in a tiny Sears mail order house in East Urbana that lacked a space for her Vipassana meditation practice. Inspired by "A Hut of One's Own," Ann Cline's philosophical hut-building chronicle, I constructed a three-tatami hut in our back garden (left). It has since become known as "Meditation Hut I" and described by Wallpaper* Magazine as "an enlightened modernist's fairytale."

When we moved into a larger Sears house closer to campus, the desire to have a special space in the new garden came with us. The result was Meditation Hut II "Le Cadeau," a second hut that I constructed. In Le Cadeau, the hand-cut shingles are wrapped around a simple archetypal "Monopoly" house frame. Despite its unorthodox flashing details, it is still water tight and has weathered nicely over the years.

These self-initiated projects were followed by opportunities to create spaces of serenity for others: Meditation Hut III "Victor," for Mary Kalantzis and Bill Cope in rural Champaign County; the ongoing projects for Kamran Fallahpour and Suzanne Kazemian Falla along Lake George in upstate New York; and the retreat cabin for Michael Andrechak and Kathy Seybert near the Illinois/Indiana border.

Each of these projects responds to the basic human desire to identify and seek creative ways to resolve the conflicts of living in the everyday world. By carefully orchestrating built form, filtering sensory input, and paying careful attention to human scale, physical space can positively impact one's emotional state. I elicit these emotional responses through the silent but materially rich medium of architecture. By carefully crafting and detailing each part so that it is part of an integral whole, I construct places of introspection and serenity, private spaces that allow people to find refuge in quiet contemplation.

Of growing interest to me are two ideals central to the Japanese tea ceremony culture as it evolved during the 16th century: the concepts of wabi (refined rusticity) and sabi (the expression of time). These two concepts have inspired many contemporary designers around the world who attempted to connect their work to nature and to humanity. In my projects, wabi-sabi is filtered through a lens of vernacular archetypes to evoke a materially rich regional aesthetic. Wabi-sabi is explicitly expressed through contrasts between weathering and non-weathering materials, tracking of sunlight and shadow along inside and outside surfaces, channeling water across roofs and walls and through scuppers, and framing specific views that record contextual seasonal changes. The material presence serves as the focus for reflection and is therefore essential to my exploration into spaces intended for their calming or contemplative properties.

As Ann Cline's book inspired me to build my first hut, my greatest hope is that this small book provides some inspiration to seek quiet spaces as a refuge from the noisy, technological world. This book is dedicated to finding the serene corner, room, or building that can stimulate direct experience, serving to evoke simple reverence for humanity and nature.

–Jeffery S. Poss

Meditation Hut I

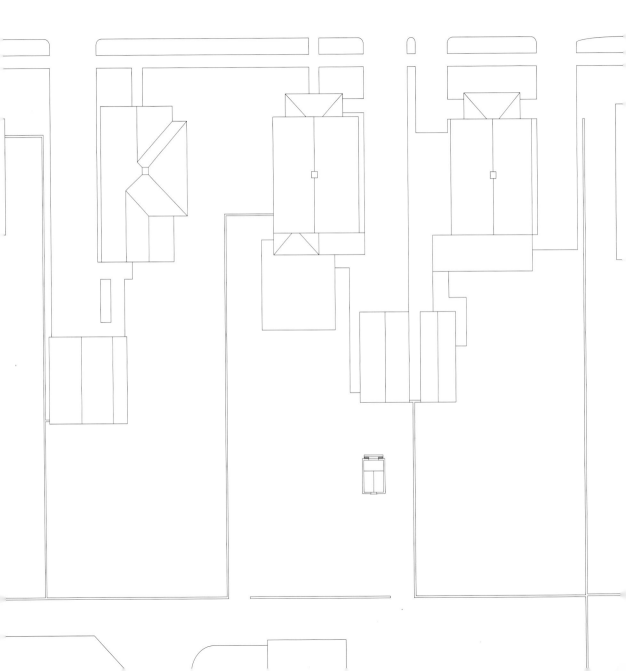

It is in the sanctuary of silent places,
with mindful attention, that the liberation
of the heart can be gained.
　　　　　　　　　　　　–Buddha

This meditation hut is located in the backyard garden of a small residence in a working-class neighborhood in east central Illinois. In its design, construction, and purpose, it was conceived as both a form and a process that encouraged the mind to focus, center, and transcend.

I completed the majority of the construction myself, clearing, digging, anchoring, framing, wiring, cladding, and finishing everything except the roof. The experience of its creation was a retreat both to and from work.

The size and proportion of a traditional tatami mat provides the human-scaled module for the floor, fenestration, and roof. The large recycled windows, coincidentally the same size as the mats, are oriented east and west. This creates a play of light and shadow across the floor and the V-shaped ceiling throughout the day.

Through material selection, formal analogy, detailing, and arrangement, architecture, landscape, and meaning are woven into a single composition. The hut is raised off the ground to allow the garden to spread underneath. Rainwater collected from the V-shaped roof fills the ground pool beneath the small casement window to nourish plant life. A fountain provides a meditative foreground sound and also masks the noise from a nearby road.

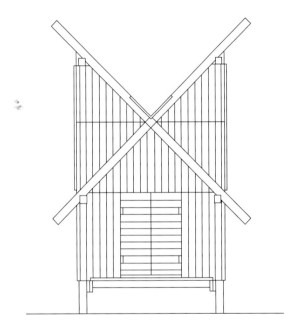

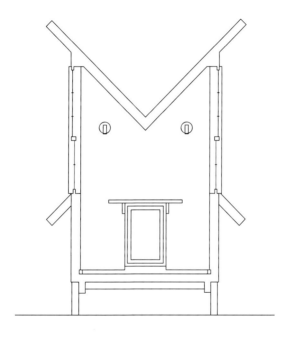

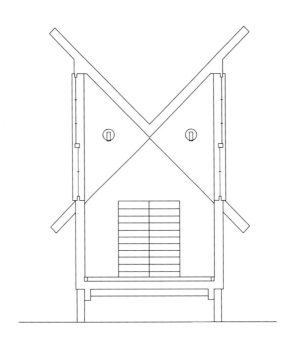

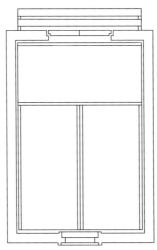

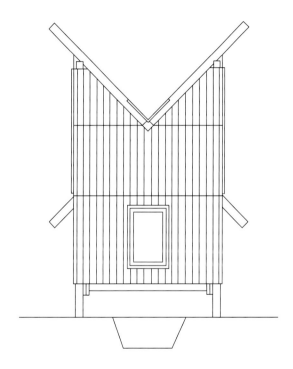

Lake George Tea Hut

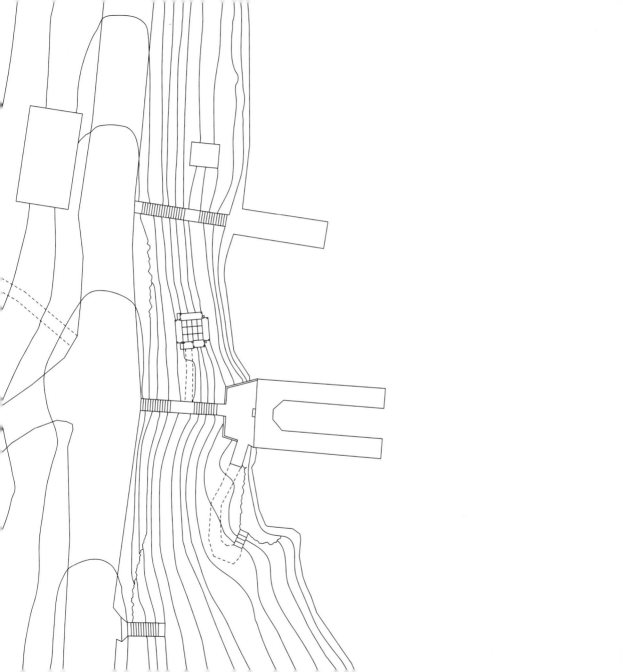

The hermit crab prefers a little shell because he knows the dimensions of his own body.

                    –Kamo no Chomei

The tea hut was designed for a vacation property along the shore of Lake George in the Adirondack region of New York. The form was derived from a series of site constraints that clarified and focused the concept. The structure rests on a tiny 8′ x 8′ concrete block foundation required by zoning standards. The locally-milled timber structure above the foundation is stained white and contrasts the black-framed insect screens. These combine with untreated, locally-milled cedar wallboards to create a series of seat niches cantilevering out from the block foundation.

This strong structural and material expression creates an interior of refined rusticity in harmony with its rural location. Openings in these niches are arranged to frame views of Lake George and provide glimpses of the adjacent contex while also carefully screening nearby distractions. It is open, yet protected. It creates an appropriate setting for an intimate conversation or a quiet cup of tea.

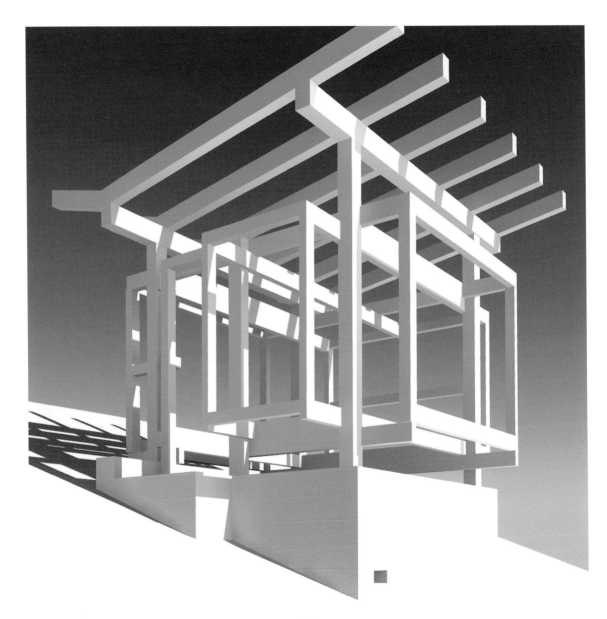

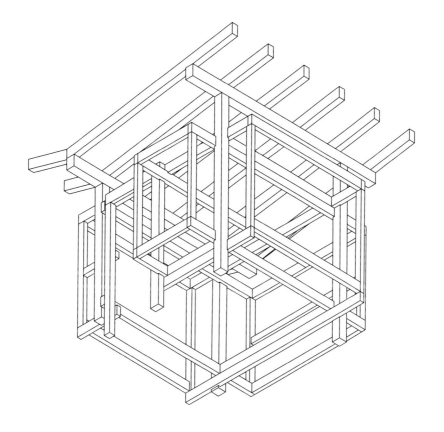

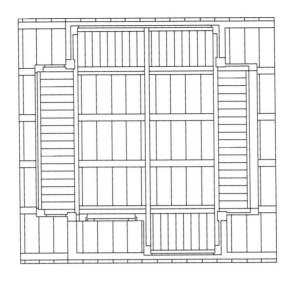

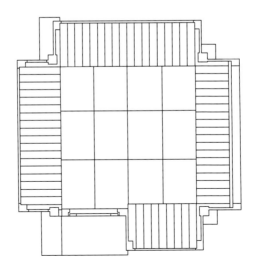

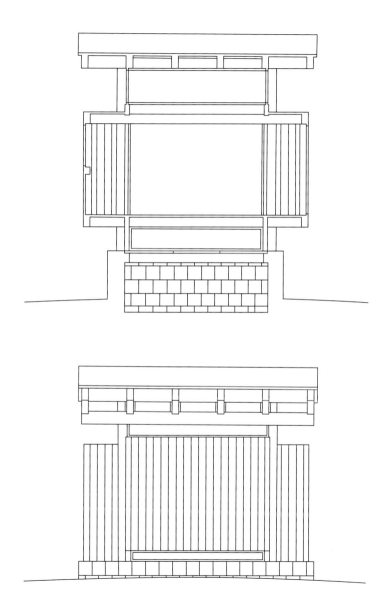

Meditation Hut II "Le Cadeau"

Everything is in process. Everything—
every tree, every blade of grass, all the
animals, insects, human beings, build-
ings, the animate and the inanimate—is
always changing, moment to moment.
                    –Pema Chodron

The hut is located in the back corner of a residential garden, nestled in a mature landscape. As with the first hut, I constructed it myself. But this time, I began without a full idea of what the resulting form would be. As it grew, decisions of space, aperture, and detail were tested and then resolved. The hands-on construction process was once again cathartic.

Much like a wrapped gift, a single material (cedar shingles) covers the entire exposed exterior surface. Under-coursing shingles were selected for their imperfect knots and crooked grain. These are layered and detailed to create a simple archetypal house shape - like a child's first attempt to represent a dwelling in drawing form - left to weather to silver gray and moss green.

The interior is unadorned, except for three tatami mats that rest on the ebony stained structural base. Reflective white walls hover above this base to create an environment of simplicity and lightness. Small windows were placed throughout the surface to cross-ventilate and frame specific views. A small aperture cut into the door frames the head of a Buddha sculpture that greets meditators along the approach path. A casement window in the lower southwest corner frames colorful plants.   Sliding windows at the top of each gable end filter dappled light into the space throughout the day. These operable apertures create an ambiance that softly resonates with the songs of birds from surrounding trees.

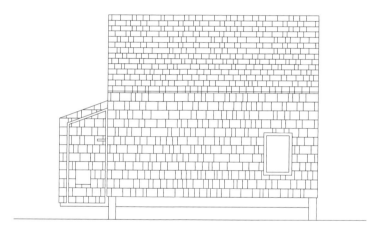

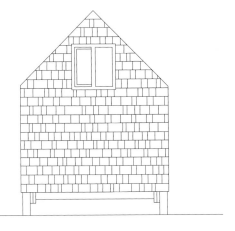

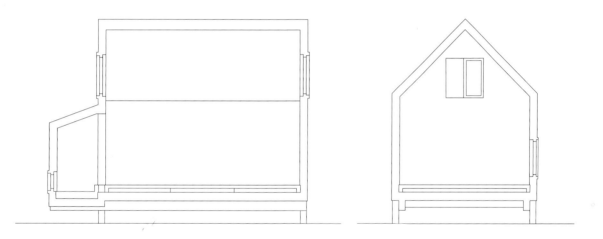

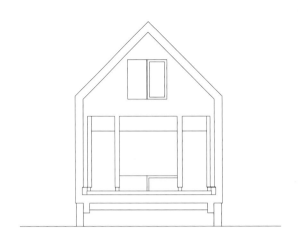

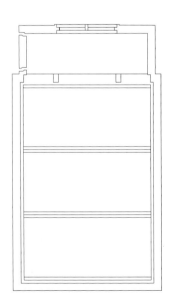

REX Retreat Cabin

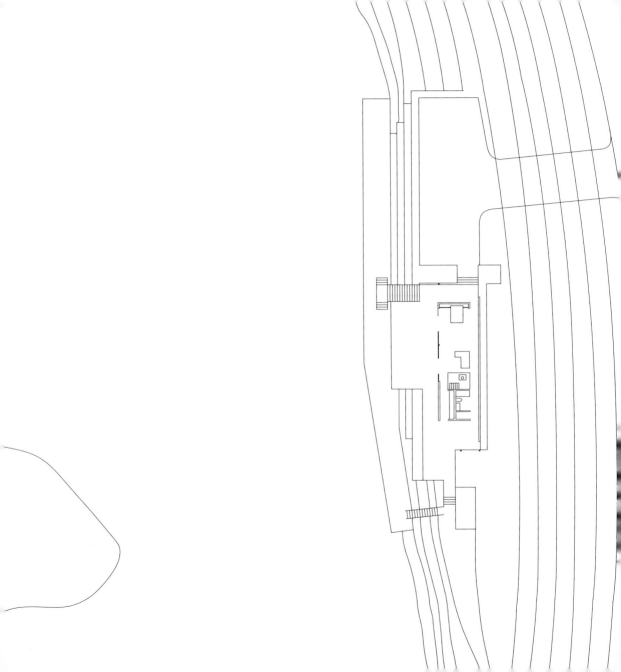

Mind peaceful, body at rest,
this is where I belong.
—Po Chü-i

"REX" is located within an extensive landscape of abandoned strip mines transformed into ponds, islands, and forest groves. The specific site is on a linear mound formed by the rock spoil surrounding a former coal mining excavation. In time, water filled the excavation and vegetation tempered the surrounding surface scars.

The building is shaped to react to its specific environment. A series of stepped and landscaped terraces connects the edge of the pond to the living levels above. Deep eaves along the entire west side shade the strong afternoon sun. The long, narrow plan is developed to maximize views and cross-ventilation. The natural, weathered exterior surfaces create a quiet backdrop for the activities of life.

The 800-sf, four-season, open plan takes full advantage of the picturesque water views that have evolved over time. The ground floor features living, sleeping, washing, and cooking spaces with framed views and multiple access points to the outdoor terraces.

In the small loft above is a sleeping and meditation space. Its semi-detached form rises away from the other program elements, opening to views, sunlight, and sounds in three directions.

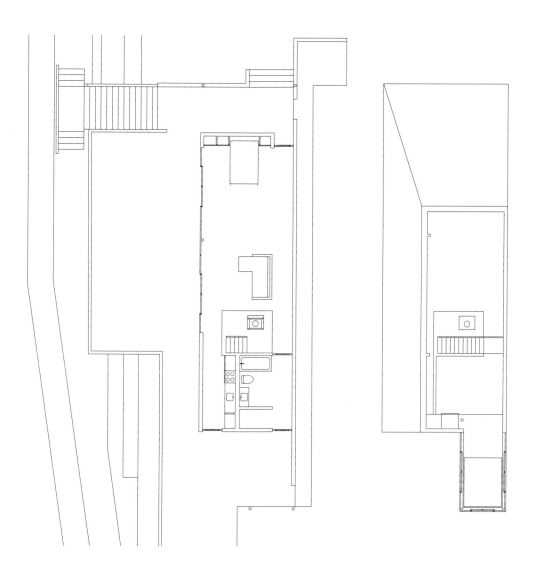

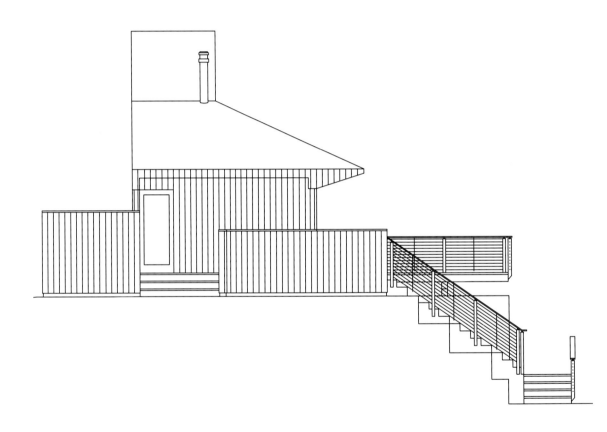

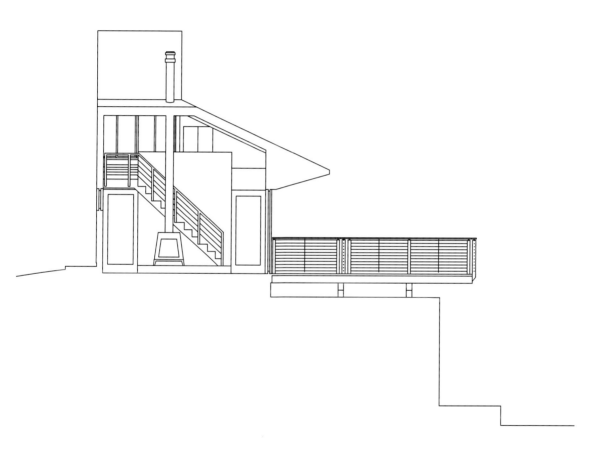

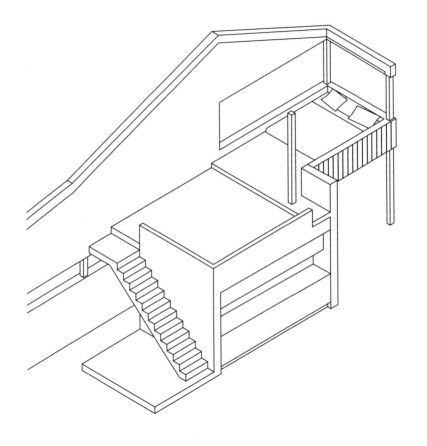

Polygon Sculpture Studio

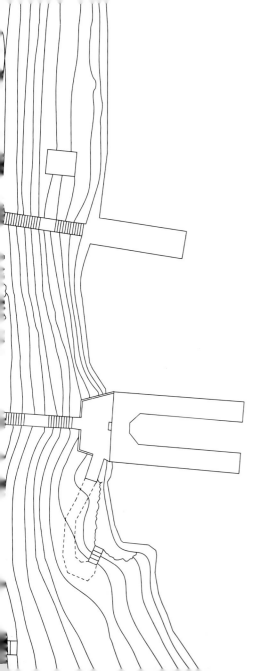

*Architectural space, however
large or small, joins and then
bends attention to new thoughts,
to a heightened consciousness.*
    –Ann Cline

The owners of a steep, lakefront property wanted a small studio for making sculpture and a loft for reflection. The form expresses these two functions.

The studio is at the highest, westernmost point of the property, 130 steps above the water's edge. The ground level is divided into a vertical, light-filled space and a service zone tucked under the loft. The loft above forms its own gabled volume. It's eastward-facing deck has tree-filtered views of Lake George.

The exterior cladding references Adirondack rural vernacular and helps emphasize the spatial conception. Galvanized steel siding wraps the gables and north end. Vertical planks of local red cedar cover the polygonal east and west sides. Cedar, introduced into the interior, creates a warm and aromatic environment. The studio has become a treasured location in which to create works of art while being immersed in the sights, sounds, and smells of nature.

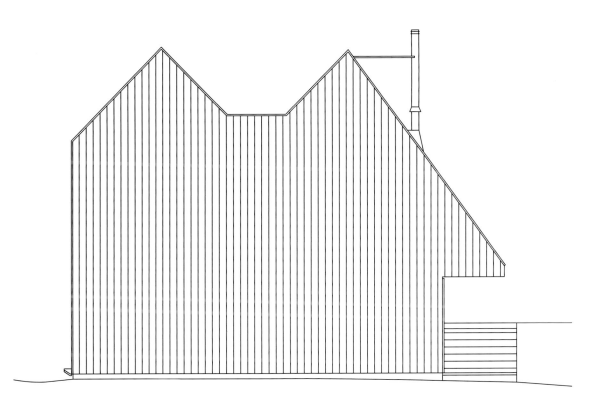

Meditation Hut III "Victor"

Meditation and water are wedded forever.
                                    –Herman Melville

The owners of a forested property wanted a quiet space to observe the surrounding nature. A naturalized understory leads to a visually kinetic approach ramp that contrasts with the subtle interior. Entry to the hut is through an obscured door detailed like the cedar walls. Inside, an oversized window opposite the entrance immediately pulls the view back outside to a composition of mature trees. Adjacent is a miniature tea cabinet. A raised platform in the main space supports three tatami mats.

The location along the north pond edge allowed the development of several aqueous experiences conducive to meditation. Throughout the day, water reflected by the sun projects onto the walls and ceiling. The roof channels rainwater to a central scupper that spills into the pond. A horizontal window in the tatami room frames a meditative view of the water. The floor of glossy ebonized birch has the sensation of a deep still pool, the grass tatami mats on the platform become an island within an island.

The result is an interior volume that is both protective and serene but alive with subtle energy. It has become the preferred place for the owners to have tea parties with their granddaughter.

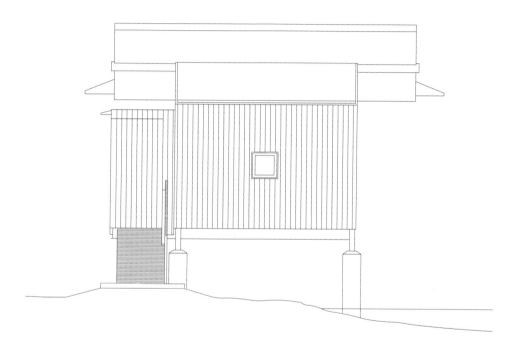

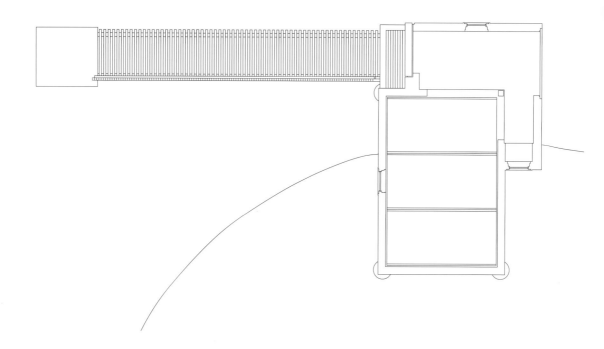

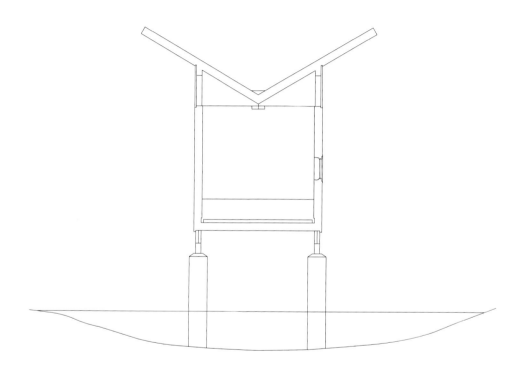

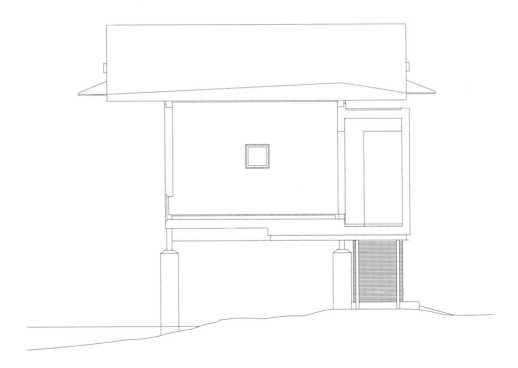

Project Information

All image credits Jeffery S. Poss, FAIA, unless noted

Prospect and Refuge
Location: Central Illinois
1991   Design: JSPA
1993   ASAP Award for Graphic
        Excellence

A House for a Subdivision
Location: Central Illinois
1992   Design: JSPA
1997   AIA Chapter Design Award

Meditation Hut I
Location: Urbana, Illinois
Client: Barbara Diller-Young
1998   Design/Construction: JSPA
2000   AIA Chapter Design Award

Lake George Tea Hut
Location: Hague, New York
Client: Kamran Fallahpour
        & Suzanne Kazemian Falla
2011   Design: JSPA

Meditation Hut II "Le Cadeau"
Location: Urbana, Illinois
Client: Barbara Diller-Young
2004   Design/Construction: JSPA
2006   AIA Chapter Design Award
2007   AIA National Small Project
        Design Award

REX Retreat Cabin
Location: Oakwood, Illinois
Client: Michael Andrechak & Kathy Seybert
2010   Design: JSPA & Workus Studio
Image credits pages 50, 54, 57, 58, 62-63: Workus Studio LLC

Polygon Sculpture Studio
Location: Hague, New York
Client: Kamran Fallahpour
        & Suzanne Kazemian Falla
2012   Design: JSPA & Workus Studio
        Construction: Robert Goetsch
        Structural: Kevin J. Wood, P.E.
2014   AIA Chapter Design Award

Meditation Hut III "Victor"
Location: Champaign, Illinois
Client: Mary Kalantzis & William Cope
2008   Design: JSPA & Jesse Haas
        Construction: Dreamworks
        Structural: PrepARE
2010   AIA Chapter Design Award
2011   AIA National Small Project
        Design Award
2014   AIA Illinois Mies van der Rohe Award
Image credits pages 90-91: Phillip Kalantzis-Cope
Image credit inside back cover: Reproduced with permission of The News-Gazette, Inc. (Permission does not imply endorsement)

Acknowledgments

I would like to thank the following for their contributions to this monograph:

Gordon Goff, for his encouragement to develop this content into a monograph;

Ryan Buresh & Evan Morris, for their insightful suggestions that brought this project to another level;

Illinois School of Architecture Director Peter Mortensen, & Environmental Arts Development Director Gail Rost, for their support of this project;

Jesse Haas & Ryan Sarros of Workus Studio, for their collaborative excellence and enthusiasm;

Mary Kalantzis & Bill Cope, for allowing me the freedom to fully realize Victor;

Phillip Kalantzis Cope, for his marvelous eye;

Kamran Fallahpour & Suzanne Kazemian Falla, for having the intuition and trust to hire a complete stranger;

Dick Williams, Jack Baker, William Eng, & Richard Betts, inspiring teachers inside and beyond the classroom;

Mom & Dad, for their eternal encouragement, allowing our house to be transformed into a construction space;

And of course, Barbara Diller-Young, muse, soul mate, disciplined hut user.

Publishers of Architecture, Art, and Design
Gordon Goff: Publisher

www.oroeditions.com
info@oroeditions.com

Published by ORO Editions

Graphic Design: Jeffery S. Poss   Edited by: Ryan Buresh & Evan Morris
Production Coordinator: Meghan Martin   Text: Jeffery S. Poss

10 9 8 7 6 5 4 3 2 1 First Edition

Library of Congress data available upon request. World Rights: Available

ISBN: 978-1-941806-84-5

Color Separations and Printing: ORO Group Ltd.
Printed in China.

International Distribution: www.oroeditions.com/distribution

ORO Editions makes a continuous effort to minimize the overall carbon footprint of its publications. As part of this goal, ORO Editions, in association with Global ReLeaf, arranges to plant trees to replace those used in the manufacturing of the paper produced for its books. Global ReLeaf is an international campaign run by American Forests, one of the world's oldest nonprofit conservation organizations. Global ReLeaf is American Forests' education and action program that helps individuals, organizations, agencies, and corporations improve the local and global environment by planting and caring for trees.